active minds

opposites

PHOTOGRAPHY
George Siede and Donna Preis

CONSULTANT
Istar Schwager, Ph.D.

Evans

Evans Brothers Limited

on

On and off,
a puppy's
new bed.

off

Consultant Istar Schwager holds a PhD in educational psychology
and a master's degree in early childhood education.
She has been an advisor for numerous child development and early learning programmes,
including the television programme Sesame Street, and has regularly written articles for parents on a range of topics.

C 1992 Publications International Ltd

First published in Great Britain in 1993 by
Evans Brothers Ltd
2A Portman Mansions
Chiltern Street
London W1M 1LE

Printed in Slovenia by DELO - Tiskarna, Ljubljana

ISBN 0 237 51322 6

off

Off and on,
a hat on
your head.

on

in

In and out,
a truck dumping rocks.

out

Out and in,
a jack-in-the-box.

out

in

front

back

Front and back,
    a fireman's hat.

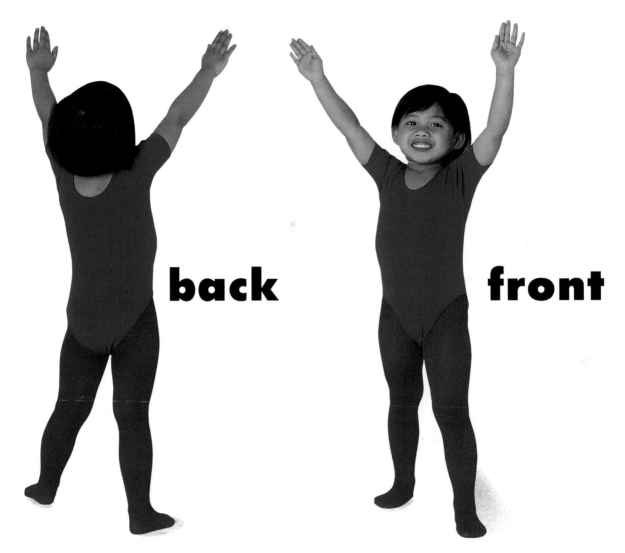

back

front

Back and front,
a young acrobat.

open

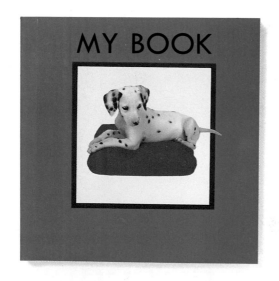

MY BOOK

Open and closed, a picture book.

closed

Closed and
open,
let's take
a look.

open

up

Up and down,
touch your
toes.

down

up

Down and up,
bounce it
goes!

down

Stop and go,
around the town.

stop

go

go

Go and stop,
now sit down.

stop

big

Big and little,
a dog and
a pup.

little

little

Little and big,
a balloon
blown up.

big

over

Over and under,
two bears are
at play.

under

over

under

Under and over,
two trains on
their way.